Introduction

I never knew I wanted to be a writer and only took up the pen after suffering a severe bout of anxiety and depression a few years ago, and that was initially to scribble in a journal every day.

In the process of that scribbling, I discovered a joy for wordplay and poetry. There's something about the power of the medium that allows me to breath and it has been profoundly healing for me.

It was a dark time back then, but I had finally found a way to express my emotions, all those thoughts and feelings that I had bottled up for years. So much of my time was spent running around working, earning money and doing little else but spending it and collapsing in front of the TV.

There is so much life and beauty in the world if only I had stopped long enough to notice it. Through mindful awareness, I have experienced a spiritual awakening of sorts that has carried and sustained me throughout my poetic journey.

I hope this collection of poetry—my first—will inspire you, that it will touch and move you, and most of all, that you will simply enjoy it. After all, it is you, the reader, who helps make all of this possible.

Winter Goose Publishing
2701 Del Paso Road, 130-92
Sacramento, CA 95835

www.wintergoosepublishing.com
Contact Information: info@wintergoosepublishing.com

Phases of the Moon

First Edition, August 2012

Cover Art by Winter Goose Publishing
Typeset by Victoriakumar Yallamelli

ISBN: 978-0-9851548-9-9

Published in the United States of America

For my sister Melanie Vasilescu

Table of Contents

Shadow Dancing

She shadow dances. She can do this;
fold up the night, paint herself black
to shut out all life, death and love.

But there is something of madness
in her vagueness, her dreams. Her soul
a blown fuse, a faint flicker of blue.

He is there, sliding under her skin,
pouring blood from the throat
of his sacrifice. He walks into her dark,

feeling its heat, the throb of it,
his tongue tracing the soft bruise
of her mouth. She knows of it now,
seen its light, high up

where the city skyline sleeps.

Where there is life, death and love.

The Scent of Warmer Rain

Maybe if I lie here
and listen to the raindrops
sweeping on the wind,
I won't think of how he stands there,
of how he has that look
or the way he strokes my hair.

If I watch the trees instead,
outlined starkly against the sky,
maybe I won't remember
how he softly leans into my body,
how he quivers in the darkness of the air.

This is how I love you,
suspended in the blueness
of the aria in my dreams,

embraced by the scent
of warmer rain.

We Talk of Weather

We talk of weather,
of how it drips
like water
through our fingers,
to the grey of rain
or snowflakes
laying softness on the night.
Like your hand folded
warm in mine.

I savour this,
this moment that can change
so suddenly
in a squeal of brakes,
shattered glass and flames—

there but for the grace of God go I

—and the autumn leaves,
even in death,
are beautiful colours
of decay.

A Warm Breath

The small cove is empty,
save for us;
a rocky, windswept place
where water laps the beach
like my night-time sea laps the shore.

We're uncertain of where to start
as the day wades through itself,
walking the surging tide
with waves licking at our feet.

I feel the tremble,
the way a river must feel a leaf
that drops on its surface,
sending ripples to the distant banks.

It's like moonlight or thunder;
sudden rain
that turns a dead world
luscious green again,

and the music plays,
carries to the firmament
to melt with Earth's song . . .

a warm breath
in a cold rush of wind.

Phases of the Moon

The child is a silhouette.

We share phases of the moon,
she and I, moving through scenes
of silvered landscapes,
fields of purple
swaying under a setting sun.

The day buckles beneath the night,
and in the trees a small bird sings.

Then, there she is
walking the asphalt lights
with jagged shards of memories
vivid on the walls of my film-screen mind,
rolling out the clips
of things that went terribly wrong.

The tone captures an essence
down in hollows of darkness and dust.

That day stole the river music,
the apprenticeship of your amber flight.

Kindling

The night is a white rush of sound,

the trees shaking in the wind
as leaves fall to a whisper,
and a crow drops out of the air.

I listen to the rattling doors,
the rushing of water outside,
needing an intimation
of beginnings, perhaps,
an untaught thing.

And I see it in your eyes,
the kindling of something fiercer.

I think, think too much.
Undress.
Lie down with this.
Unravel.
Like the cloud-rushed sky.

Traces

I sit in river sunlight
bathing under summer's final breath,
a woman-child, lost in dreams again.
A confetti of birds startle,
a cacophony of sound,
the wind spinning closer and louder,
rain beading from the sky.

Waiting forever, it seems,
for a single moment to arrive,
watching thoughts, desires,
tangling with the reeds,
spinning guilty secrets
in a glistening, luminous tail.

Nocturnal traces linger
and he is there
with cinnamon in his eyes.
He turns to her.
A spark is lit.
They are close, entwined,
kissing that slow-tongued kiss;
two circles sucked beneath the waters,
dissolved into clouds.

Night Moth

At twilight,
as day melts away,
trembling with heat and flame,
ghosts appear as visions,
white as bone glinting in the darkness.

Between the moon and streaming water,
a night moth flits
in the bright excluding circle
shining beside my bed.

It is a mere wisp of life,
a gift, some small grace
to join me in the blackest night.

I feel its flutter, its heartbeat breath,
and I long to join its flight,
my arms ready, open for the lift,
lost in some memory of a dream,
the sheer weight of it.

It died, of course.
I woke at dawn
to gather up its wings.

Whale Song

They say there are whales
still roaming the furthest waters
that stretch from here to deepest blue,
and all the way to infinity.

Sometimes I hear their voices,
a pulsating echo passing back and forth
before the lifting wind
drowns them beneath its heavy swell.

Come morning, the tide rises
as I collect the shells the ocean has left
to remind us of the song slipping from earth's
fading light, its music forever lost.

Wings Over Waters

I witness
the delicate curves
of wonder in motion,
wings across waters of rebirth,
as high, as wide, as an ocean.

A union
of reality and dreams,
fingertips touching the stars.
An hourglass whispers
of a conscious existence.

This

For months you spent
your time in darkness,
laid out against a heavy sun,
as the purest blue
filtered through an open window.

You did not sleep
and would not for days yet,
cloistered and claustrophobic,
wrapped in a wingless gloom.

One morning you woke,
scattering thoughts like poppies
bowing to the wind.
"Let's make love to the rain," you said,
commanding the sunlight back to bed.

I looked up at the sky, amazed—
it was your light,

our light—

this.

River Music

There is something about this music
that sets me dreaming
as the day turns on a wing-tip
in afternoon light.

A mad sun is laughing;
I feel its touch on my newly
cracked skin. He is with me
yet not, listening to this song.

The notes sing of harmony
in the dancing air of midnight,
weaving me through with new hope,
rendering me purer of sound.

Harvest

Down the lane by your mother's house,
we stopped to taste the berries
growing there, bushes bursting,
ripe and ready to be picked.
A prelude to a bitter frost perhaps,
but we didn't care, filling our mouths
with summer, fingers darkening
with their juice. We held the roots
to feel the water swell, tongues lapping
at the streams from the sky.
Later we found some apples;
left a bruise around the tree
while we scavenged for their sweetness,
cinnamon and sugar on our breath
and sap rising beneath our skin.

Starry Nights

He sighs as the full moon rises,
spilling wings of tarnished silver
through the midnight trees.

He lies against the wall,
still shiny and wet
from nights spent underwater.

Jupiter winks an eye,
too far away to touch,
hovering in stranger skies.

A whisper in the mind
is full of constellations,
stars vivid in their brightness.

Dreams become the swallows
swooping to a grainy dawn.

Wind Chimes

In full sunlight
by an ancient banyan tree,
a half-wild girl falls in love,
in a ceremony
of worship, sacrifice,
resurrected ghosts.

Faces swim in a languid motion
through the dancing flames of fire,
while every branch has an eye
fixed on ochre-painted skin.

Hot winds tangle with a butterfly
perched on a bird-of-paradise flower.
This, their consecrated temple;
the womb, this universe.

The Dance

Blue is the mood that crackles the room,
my clothes strewn across your floor.

The air holds me as you do,
with naked hands, a touch so light.

You are behind me, everywhere at once,
watching endless eyes fading into the gloom.

Dusk wraps its wisps around my limbs
and I'm breathing fast,
listening to the vibrating winds
splash the sky with brilliant hues.

I lose the enemy of the child inside.
Your touch,
a silken tendril along my skin.

Night Lover

To drink his blood;
vampiric lust, life essence lost.

To see his eye colour change my colour;
dusk darkened, vitality sucked.

So pale his cheek, paper-cool his touch.
His shadow deep,
crueller than winter's frost.

Blood of the living feeds my lover,
my sadistic brother,

my him and me.

Shadows of You

Words drip from my pen,
oozing from the growing dusk
as restless night creeps in
across the shadows of you
sleeping there in silent seas.

With sensuous lips apart
we dive through swirling waters,
dormant passion wakening
to the tune of a lullaby,

each passing note
becoming a purer sound.

A Thousand Links

A thousand links
but no connections,
cast adrift in the sea.
It's cold and I shiver.
Smokey air
stains the summer sky.
Hypnogogic voices
whisper unrequited love
(if love it was)
now just ignored.
All the lies,
all there ever was
with nothing in between.
A heap of bones
and a chasm
for you to jump across.

Oceans Apart

I lie here watching the dark
overshadow the day,
listening to the rise
and fall of your breath,
tasting your lingering kiss,
the length of your body against mine.

Somehow the night has grown cold
as rain blows through the silence
to scatter against glass
like shattered dreams that fell
on empty wet streets.

They fall heavy and wasted,
littering the path that started
at the end of another life.
I kick them away with the leaves,
a new life beginning,
oceans apart from the past.

Sleeping Stones

I sit at my desk exhaling breaths
of nervous reality,
seeming not to care
as the computer hums,
the telephone ringing through the air.

The sounds I send
echo to my last footfall,
and the clouds racing by
to the ticking of my wristwatch,
the minutes, hours, days
of my life
etched into the cracks of the wood.

A world of complexity
spinning in orbit
a thousand miles high,
where the mountains rear
and collapse, wounded,

and I, staring at the void,
disturb my sleeping stones.

Absence

A sudden clap of wings
on an empty stretch of road,

startles me awake. I feel dizzy,
pain makes the outlines shimmer.

Sleep is my lover now,
my opiate oblivion. I want nothing

but an endless slumber, rolling
days into a timeless stream;

past hunger, vanity or caring,
to suffocate all my dreams.

Your absence is as present
as a dark bird on a windowsill.

Monday

Another workday,
another soul
dissolves,
drips
w
a
t
e
r
along the windowpane,
sinking
unseen
to silence,
drowning.

Please bring me floods and earthquakes,
bring me night.
Bring me solar winds
and give me strife.
Bring me twisted love
and yearning.
Bring me life.

Catching Moondrops

The boy picks his way
from the edges
of the poorer part of town,
catching morning light
and brushing moondrops
from his skin
that seeped through gaps
between the leaves
of the tree that loomed above him.

As he checked the stars
his hand brushed against the bark,
finding some connection
with the branch carved into a man,
bringing comfort and some light
into his dark.

Rather like the tourists
who gave him some change,
wanting him to go
before he spoiled
their holiday snaps.
They knew he'd never leave.

Today, he didn't need to raid the trash cans
that sat outside the people's houses,
the precious scraps they threw away,
that keep him alive.

He turns his face up to the sky
to catch a ray of sun
and dreams of living,
if only for the day.

The Soldier

The soldier fights a war every day,
the enemy and elements of a foreign land.
He takes the cold, the heat,
the rain and sandstorms
that close around him,
clinging like the stench of fear
he felt when the boy appeared,
not more than twelve,
carrying death in his hand,
exploding into entrails
glistening by the roadside.

Covered in dirt, sweat and blood
he slumps against a wall,
unwashed, unshaven,
and pulls out the picture
of his pretty wife, their child
who reminds him of the boy,
the innocence reflected in his eyes.

He will come this way again,
to the intersection of a moment,
as he patrols disfigured streets
full of hatred for his kind.

On this winter's morning,
the sun throws its web of light
across the fields of home.

Fate

In between the mountain tops,
below a sky of crystal blue,
lie the valleys of fresh green grass
and leaves blossoming on the trees.

A long, slow moving stream
wends its way around the pass,
following bends and curves
as far as the eye can see.

Streams of refugees are returning home,
piling their belongings high
on tractors, donkey carts,
arriving back to burnt out houses,
broken lives forever torn apart,
their daughters raped
and beaten, their sons lined up to die.

My eyes catch those of a little girl
sitting on her mother's lap.
She looks at me and I at her.
I smile and she smiles back,
raising an arm to wave.

Would she ever know
that I'm reminded of my daughter?
That she has the same colour in her eyes?

Destiny has put her there.
Fate decides who suffers

and who will never know
how luck is on their side.

Food for Thought

Men carry guns into the famine zone,
hide from Unicef. We will be marked

by this, they say, ten thousand already
dead, as elders discuss the lack of rain.

Another child dies, wrapped in a sheet;
the darkness seeps in the pools of his eyes.

Travellers tire of crying, walking the miles
where the ancients once dwelled.

Out on the plain, dust swirls in the wind,
falls on the heads of cattle, the few that remain.

Empty

He watches as the crows
fall to the trees
standing empty
against a darkening sky.

As dusk descends,
there he is, alone
where painful memories reside,
staring out the window,
wondering where earth ends
and heaven or hell begins,
or if they exist at all.

The light falls on his face,
on the lines etched into his skin,
like marks of his soul
that can never be erased.

Why does the smile
never reach the greyness of his eyes?

What She Sees

I wonder what she sees
whilst staring at the blankness
of the middle distance,
a space of starless nights,
streaks of shadows
cutting across her weightless sight.

This is her death, the way she dies,
yet somewhere in that broken mind
she breathes a restless sigh.

I wonder at her choice,
preferring numbness over life.
Her healing burns;
she feels the pain it gives.

If she knew what I knew,
would she choose to live?

Sunday Morning

On Sunday morning
silence lands
in a world of sleep,
as rain pit patters to a halt
and the sun peeks out.

Among the calm
two birds take flight,
beating wings
to the rhythm
of your half sleep,
scattering air-brushed blessings
feather-soft against your cheek.

You roll over
mumbling to your lover's side,
trailing hands along his back,
connecting in a way
that tilts the angle
of the earth,

light to dark
and back again,

to the beginning
of the story,
bookmarked
to when the rainbow
climbed above your heads.

Star of Peace

Violence explodes. In America,
bodies fall into fire, dust and darkness.

Felt the blast as the plane went down.
We can hardly believe we're here

says the fireman, skin wrenched
from bone. In Afghanistan, villagers

flee in fear. A jet plane screams
overhead. Streams fire from the sky.

Can hardly write of holy wars or death.
We light a star of peace for everyone.

A Hard Rain

Can you hear it,
the scent of fear
running on the wind?
That's the sound of the axe
that's bleeding, dripping blood
of the local community.

They are selling off our dreams,
the one's you and I once had,
for the public good, they say,
though the politician's lying.

They've ripped out the heart
of an apathetic nation.
The banker has his cash.
It's the poor and sick
who'll have to pay it back.

What happened to those days,
the times that were a-changin'?

The Children Know

It is winter, near to freezing
as I walk the winding pathway
by the rising river waters.
All is silent but for the hush
as a kestrel hovers overhead,
swooping down with wings unfurled,
eyes fixed on unsuspecting prey.

And I feel a sudden flush of love
for this, for life, for us,
like a spark of something bigger
than myself, a flash of inspiration
in my exhaled breath,
spinning like the wooded scented earth
in the early mist of light.

I'd forgotten, or only half recalled
what the children already know
about the sky, its deepest blue.

Morning Glory

Morning light attacks
the sweat of yesterday
still clinging to my skin
as I emerge
flapping into being,
shocked by dazzling white.

Ecstatic, I hear echoes
of the children dancing
under scented apple trees,
full of foetal
half formed thoughts,
laden with fruit uneaten.

The Gloaming

Out in the late half light
where the underworld
lies in darkness,
an owl blinks
its oval, gold-rimmed eyes,
paused and still,
watching for some creature
of the dusk,
lifting from the branch
to glide on silent wings
softer than the silken moth,
lighter than the night.
Just one passing feather,
like the falling snowflakes
on the frozen land,
delivers a bitter kiss.

The Song Never Sung

The rain came,
time stopped
breathing,
leaves fell inside me
blown along a
temporal flow
of images
lining up the shore,
with arms held high
then sinking—

as autumn claimed
its ghost,
beauty met
a tidal flood.
Mountains grew,
shadows lengthened
into a song never sung.

Love visited
and then was gone.

Prayer

Prayer is like the kingfisher
that you long to see
but rarely do,
yet when you least expect it,
a flash of brightness
in a sudden spark of blue.

Midwinter

The dead end of year
looks towards another frost,
wintry sunlight glancing
through the sleepy trees
standing there tall and stark,
bare of the fading fire reds
and golden hues of their dying leaves.

It's getting late and as the wind
whips across my face,
the sun sinks behind a hill
swallowed in a sudden rush,
and I reflect on the wondrous birth
at the darkest centre of this season.

The day God became a man to die,
to change the pattern of the stars,
the moon, the shadows beneath my skin.

Little Owl

The little owl sits on the weathered
dry stone wall,

sheltered in a fold behind a purple-covered hill.
Before me, the land

stretches to the Atlantic shore itself,
the wind blowing on the edge of afternoon.

He flies up as he sees me

meeting the wind and dancing,

wings beating a rhythm in my chest
as I drop

from my life's complexities

into his.

Seeing Zebras

Real time seems eternal
or instantaneous,

either way, outside of *now*
where patterns of colour

through bevelled glass
fall across my desk, my hand.

In my underlying consciousness
lies linear time,

full of yesterday and tomorrow,

flowing through heart and lungs,
through endless breath

where love is earth's glow off its edge.

The Sound of River Water

You sit there searching
a heart of emptiness,

the sun and its reflection
throwing shadows

to the sound of river water
dripping beneath the storyline

of your day, your life,
to the real meaning below,

where it pools in depths
after falling rain.

You can hear the sea,
touch the star-like shapes

and know it in your bones,
your newly opened darkness

where you lean into the hush
of things unseen inside

and tell your stories to the wind.

Midnight Lights

It is the witching hour
and we are out
crossing the fields from the road.

There's a strangeness in the sky,
moonshine through your skin.

Shadows fall through trees
like crows circling the night,
sucking each breath from me

as stillness hangs
in this in-between world.

A fox slips suddenly from the woods
while we watch,
pressed close together,
the dream, a glimmer in the dark.

Awakening

I see him yet don't understand
how it is he holds onto joy
during moments in time
when the spark seems like it is dying,

carrying me along on a cloudburst,
away from the grey and mechanic
into the poetic and extraordinary.

To a place where the ice is melting,
where fire has raged through the forests,
where the river flows on like electricity.

So often I awake on the edge of a word
tethered to the wind. To nothing.

Remnants

I was born bewildered,
half elsewhere

in trees that glittered
at dawn after the rain fell.

You climbed my curves
with gentle hands in tears.

I feared for you then,
afraid you could fall

through skies awash
with pinks and blues

as my tiny fingers clutched
at tattered remnants of another life.

You crept along my branches
paving pathways to different worlds,
beyond the otherness of broken minds.

How far I have travelled from that place,
embarrassed by my vulnerability,

trembling in the sunlight,
a metamorphosis of a kind.

Gravestones

In the corner of a quiet afternoon
among the wind, the trees and birds,
I walk to where I read and think,
to let the silence speak
and listen to the ghosts
who haunt this peaceful place.

There are secrets left in death,
fragments of a story, poems to recite.
They once had dreams and hopes,
ideas of lazy Sunday mornings
lying in bed with faces soft from sleep,
weekday jobs and bank accounts,
morning tea and toast.

Some graves are old, cold,
overgrown with grass,
here since 1851.
The ever-changing weather's
beaten down the stone,
the inscription that read
He was a much-loved son.
Now a century or more
has been and gone.

The cemetery is altered by the seasons;
not much happens here
except the rain and summer days,
history repeating itself.
The wind picks up, scatters blossom

from the cherry trees across the graves
where loved ones once tended to their dead.

Daylight turns, the clouds call me home.

The Thaw

It's on mornings like these
that I feel the air,
the wings beating against my chest
as though I've been here before,
along the fields of snow
with no one there,
below a lavender sky
that turns a deeper blue.
The sun glints on white
untrodden paths, over
streams that melt and bubble
with my own heart,
like the voice of a bird,
its song, a flower inside the ice.

Dreaming

It started as I was floating
on the surface of waking,
whirling in an updrift
over landscaped dreams,
somewhere lost in time.

Swimming was like flying
and the fish were birds
spinning moonless into midnight,
breathing easily in the air,
possessing nothing, not even weight.

And crowded in my eyes,
the shape of a winged form
with heartbeats to the tune of mine
as I lay stricken
like a sheep upon its back.

Afterwards I awoke
to fragments, silence, sky.

Silence

Let me alone, as
gentle winds in silence blow
evanescent dreams

Debris

She sits sipping a glass of red,
glancing out the window of a wine bar,
considering the emptiness of her world,
watching time passing by.
Her mobile rings and she fumbles,
rifling through the debris
of her busy, cluttered life.
The screen flashes with an urgency,
a buzz; she answers *hello*.
Outside, the sky changes colour,
a burst of light, an outstretched hand.
She bites her lip, uncertain as to why
the moon brings out the ghosts of night.

Fireweed

How long is a moment?
The second when our gazes met;
a brush of wind from the ocean bed,
a seagull's cry. And the air?
It shimmered above our heads,
an electric river flowing
as words were left unsaid.

I think I'm drowning,
clear waters fill my mouth,
fireweed brushes against heavy legs.
Too close the river's edge,
sunlight dancing on the surface,
strong currents beneath

pulling me below
to where the fish are dying.
Dead fingers laid on lips.
So cold
curled up with autumn leaves,

and I'm dreaming all I heard,
all you might have said.

The Angels

I built a dome for you in air,
slept deep on colours of your skies,
stroked tongues made flesh across your mind,
murmured whispers on skin laid bare.
Ghosts wailed and wept at my despair,
souls long dead stirred to haunting cries.
Man lives in sleep, asleep he dies,
bathed in tears . . . often unaware.

Tonight

On some distant shore where only she walks,
the universe hangs in a starry, endless sleep.

A piano rests on the sand like a question
she never answered, never cared to ask

afraid as she was of darker nights
thrumming through the curtains on the wind.

Her mind is coloured by what it sees
reflected back at her, the scarlet reds

of passionate lips,
the ocean blue against the skyline.

Tonight she'll dance the Tango,
her soul in knots of sinew, flesh and bone.

The First

First came the feathered birds
from wilderness and thorns,
from the age of perpetual rain
where they sang of mountains,
receding glaciers, the rocks
where the river ends.
Hopping from leaf to leaf
over clumps of silver lichen,
they told me in the purest voice
of how deep the sea is, how big the sky.
I listened from under an ashen tree
ignored by the gazes of passersby,
hidden in an afterglow of thought,
the weather seeping through my mind.

The Raven

The land leans in to block out the wind
while we head west across the island,

cracking bush twigs where we walk,
breaking the secrets of a damp,

capricious earth. A squirrel darts
between the trees and I tell it to your eyes,

this longing that mingles with my blood,
dissolving with the leaves.

You check the twisted branches
placing hands against the bark.

It was like talking to the woods, you said.
Did you not see the raven?

I smile and think of how the woodpigeon
flies a parabola in the sky.

Doubt

This is how it is:
moonlight, fragments, mirrors,
fingers tracing empty space,

hanging on a question mark
faded into nothing,
blankness, shadowed shapes.

Cold days of discontent,
no words, just silence
dripped through nights
that come from winter,
snowstorms, elemental ice.

I see it now,
feel its cold embrace,
an insistent, hissing snake.

Today . . .
I don't look back.

Poetry

Poetry is illusions tied to grace,
doubts that thread a line
between what is and isn't real,
like shadows under moonglow,
the cold shimmer of the stars.

It flies its elemental course
in fragments of a convoluted self,
the ache within a wound
that never heals,
the longing never satisfied.

No matter; hope comes in time,
reflecting warmth through daydreams,
in sunlight from the East,
the world balanced on a blade of grass.

Love lies beyond my naked poetry.

Hidden Threads

A woman, very old, lives in a book,
pages aged by air, neglected, unread.

She has wings unopened,
scars hidden in unsuspecting places,

where she would sing of trees,
the woods, the heartbeat of a poet

whose words woven in the threads
were discarded by the world.

You can see her soul if you look,
glowing visible, exposed.

And once seen, she'll never go away,
remaining in your mind, a dream.

Poet

I know my name
in this world of hierarchy,
my place passed down
through generations,
history savoured with every sentence,
every breath I take.
Oh, me of little faith
who struggles against the tides
of nights I never sleep.
I need to describe it,
articulate all that dumbfounds me
with poetry and words.
What name defines me?
Woman, dreamer, poet.

Vanilla

Hushed stillness, days when by a river,
a blade of light falls across the water,
soft dew-drop kisses,
the leaves turning golden in the park.
For this the wandering thoughts,
the fire in the dark. I give you this:
my fruit for you to eat, my flesh, the bite of it.
And then the dawn, the deep blue-gold of sky,
that burns the woody scent
emanating from your breath,
to the eruption of our circumstance.
I am helpless, initiated by your warmth
to the twists, the tremors, the stars.

Hunter's Moon

She has a soul split apart,
wrinkles line her face
defending her from
disintegration, loss.
She hears the portent
of a coming storm,
the leaves that tremble
as if for a god,
and in the changing light
she looks across the woods
to the wolf lying, waiting
in the deeper grass.

She can, to my mind,
take the night
and all its glittering stars.
A river runs right through her
taking shelter in the valleys,
in the peaks, the twists and turns,
then dipping into softness
when she talks about the water
trickling through the trees,
unfurling in the morning dew.

The darkness lands like an empty glass
narrowing ever inward,
threading deeper into artery and vein,
between the sun and the hunter's moon.

Ocean

The sea is a perfect blue,
solitary and wide.
Its silvered surface lies
as smooth as sleep,
and at the shallow edge
a young girl hesitates,
curious about its depths.
Her outline sharpens,
her bird-heart silhouetted
against the fading light.
Vague clouds spiral across the sky
and life has yet to open or be defined.
Next year, everything will change,
turn around in the cycles of the moon.
I fear for her—

Be gentle with her ocean.

The Salmon

The salmon, pink
and silver,
leaps through air
leaving behind the colder seas,
entering warmer waters
in our estuaries, our streams.
She flips and swims
to a place she knows
from memory,
spawning deep in the riverbed,
in the light
that glitters through the trees.
She is the spark of life,
where it all starts and ends.
She is the mother,
the children sleeping in their beds.

Footprints in the Snow

Time stands between us,
the rainbow crossing seas
to where our bodies meet
between a draught of air and sun.
There are moments in the dusk;
a cloud of starlings
switching through the trees
in a streak of river light.
I leave the warmth, the fire,
its orange, settling glow,
so I can bring this back,
your veracity that leads
to deeper waters,
your stride for every two of mine.
I see your tread and follow,
leaving footprints in the snow.

Not Quite Believing

Tonight the dusk that's creeping in
beneath the curtains chills my face
with cold, and I am tired once again.
The forest along the skyline
wears pale peach against grey mist,
then deeper aubergine
discloses what I feel yet cannot see,
the river's distant banks,
the gaps in between. The icy waters
lie as still as glass, though the fish
even at midnight swim and feed,
and every turn of leaf pulls me down
to crash into the next thing, the twists
and turns of love, the glitter in the dark.
Perhaps in that silence with earth
lying underneath, I will let time fall
from an empty tree and allow the world in,
not quite believing, but imagining and free.

Spider Threads

Nothing seems so easy as this,
the sizzling magenta shades
of hot summers spent lying poolside
in midday heat.
A spread lizard bathes
along the sun-baked garden wall
as pale you sit
absorbed by the churning cicada calls,
the rustle in the leaves and sticks.
A hazy lull hangs on your breath
like silver spider threads
that stretch to angles of perfect symmetry.
But in your sun-blind blink
you catch the fly, its writhes and twists,
its spinning death, and ponder
on a life not lived and all the words for love.

Dreamwalker

Always in dreams
like an early film star
from the days of black and white,
I sleepwalk through the woods
strung with nothing but the moon,
tracing circles with my footsteps,
drowning under starlight.

The rustling trees are shrouded
by the river mist descending
in the darkness of the air,
and underfoot, a sea of flowers
almost white as I turn,
luminous under a lonely glare
shining in the half light.

There is nothing here—
except for a line of tracks
leading nowhere but into dark.
Where are the night creatures,
the bat and owl? Do I walk alone?
Ghosts will surely cross this way.
I will trail in the shimmer as they pass.

Summer Snow

Just where the night begins
is where my head
weaves its web
of thought and feeling
deep below the skyline.

And then it quickly turns,
twists into a tangled thing,
into a mind that kills me
whenever my daylight ends.

My inner being is neither
cruel nor kind, a survival tool
that few know as well as I.

If I let it, it would eat at me,
catch me dying slowly
in its spinning thread,
a forever hole of thought and sense.

Off balance in the wind
my sky's a darker red.

Good morning, shadow,
it is your quiet I wish to learn,
your silence
in the sweetest summer snow.

Shattered

I can tell you how it will be—

it begins somewhere on the ocean bed;
the sky's unstable,
freak weather blows the sleet about

and the air collapses on itself,
the wind sucked in,
the storm breaking over us.

It takes us to the brink,
this something that's so immense,
so near the sea is snapping at the bank.

Yet, the room is brash with daylight,
tastes of early morning and river silt.

Earth turns, wobbles on its axis
as a dark wave arches,
shatters into pieces overhead.

Forest Creatures

A full moon hangs in the garden,
the night-time world lit by stars
and wrapped in shadows
behind a back street
away from the tapestry of lights,
the passing cars.
I go to bed to soothe myself,
keep the curtains open for a wisp of air,
a certain sense of reality, a breathing in of light.
I feel the breeze, my salty skin,
mouth and I focus on a space
where the town is lined with trees.
And while I dream, the meaning
eludes me still, the signs forever lost.
I see the forest creatures,
their outlines real against the dark,
against the glitter of the universe
that pulls me down, panting in the night.

Inner Child

I am sure she is there
behind the door, hiding
when I think I've heard her
in the awkwardness of a stranger's
voice. I see her on the stairs
and know she is my childhood
cloaked in moth wings and dust.
She trips down present-day halls,
corridors that smell of emptiness,
the breath of early life.
She thinks she is invisible
and I will keep her secret,
let her slip away again,
a soap bubble dissolving in the air.

Broken

So now it's broken,
shattered into a thousand pieces,

and she could have fixed it
before the lights came on

but she fell a thousand feet
through stars and liquid tears,

and the darkness of the room
became the milky white of blindness.

Moments in Time

I.
A vision from her past
comes back to haunt her;
he sits there
with a crumpled letter in his lap,
coffee growing cold in his hand.
He's staring into space,
has a haunted look
that Sian has seen before.
She looks up to smile
but he doesn't notice;
she thinks she'll finish late tonight.
Outside, the sparrows
gather in the dusk,
flutter in the leaves.
A cat crouches,
eyes gleaming in the dark.

II.
Time opens, closes;
Jack breaks into a sweat,
reads the letter
that's burning in his hand.
Cold light stabs his eyes
from the strip-light overhead,
but the waitress is a pretty thing;
he watches
as she wipes the table tops.
In the distance
someone plays a sax

like they're making love
to the music,
and it carries over rooftops
as twilight descends.
He takes a sip of coffee,
stands and leaves a tip,
listening as he turns to go.

III.
Dawn crests in waves
over a perfect lilac sky
of cotton clouds, soft breezes
that sweep across the cherry-blossom trees.
Jack cracks an eye,
wonders what the world
might offer him today,
though amazed he's still alive,
all muscle, sinew still intact,
but can't recall such heaviness,
the dull ache he feels inside.

Somewhere in the house
a telephone rings.
He hears her voice, sees her smile,
wishes he could find a way
past the awkwardness of office talk,
the group of children
chattering like starlings
waiting at the bus stop.
He would go where she went
in boundless silence,
with a million memories floating by.

To Where a Name Could Reach

The day turns, pulls its shadows in
along the distant mountain peaks
where twilight shivers with the stars
much further than a name could reach.
And earth attempts to heal herself
beyond the woods, the winding creeks.
The moon hangs, irresistible.
A cold wind slices through my cheeks.

Goodbye

I will give myself to the sky,
see the world as it always was,
reach for the winds that talk to me.

Pattern the shape of things to come,
in colour, sound and thoughts;
sit on the edge of starless nights.

Be the child dancing in a dream
and see the past in your tearless eyes,
ponder on your coward's kiss.

And be pleased to know you,
to never kill the thing I love.
I shall give myself to the sky.

The Little Poem That Could

The little poem grew and grew,

becoming whispers on the wind,
clouds scudding across a timeless sky.

Letters fluttered like butterfly wings
whirling in an up-drift over storm-tossed seas.

The ancient blood in forgotten words
were desires bound together, two as one.

And buried in a grave of ash,
blossoming into shoots of green,

was a legend—a little poem that could.

Destiny's Hand

I find I can't breathe
under these city lights,

replacing the stars
that shine in gentle disarray.

The night lies still and quiet;
no burning bridges,
no sea to wash me away.

He tells me to show them
who I really am,

to hold tight to destiny's hand.

I will keep the car's engine running,
ticking over, just in case.

The Night I Met a Dragon

It was an evening like any other,
starred with starlings
and approaching winter,
bird-clouds in the dark.
My heart thumped in its chest
as if for a lover, frozen in the shadows,
the hairs rising on my neck.
That was when I saw him,
a dragon with moonlight glinting off his eyes.

He whispered soul into my ear,
his own large heart
pulsing in and out of view.
I wondered, what had this creature seen,
coming from moss and mountains,
from the sea? As he flew away
with threads of blue veining
through his wings, I closed my eyes
to let the silence reassemble
itself around me, to feel the grass
waving slightly in the breeze.

I was still there at dawn,
until I heard the blackbirds sing,
their intoxicated song of morning
drowning out the distant cars.

Fragments

To the light
a little piece of me
floats away,

a snowflake, a feather,

never to be touched,
burning brightly

on a silver wheel of stars—

swept up on love's stream,
dripping velvet voices,

amalgamated pebbles
dancing on the tongue—

a distant heaven, my dream.

About the Author

The beautiful county of Somerset in Southwest England serves as perpetual inspiration for Louise Hastings and her sensuous poetry, which contemplates the connections between the human psyche and the allure of our natural world. Louise allows her thoughts and emotions to breathe through the power of her artistic expression, creating a profound healing for both the mind and the soul.

Follow Louise as she continues her poetic journey.

http://louisehastings.net

Lightning Source UK Ltd.
Milton Keynes UK
UKOW051440010313

207018UK00006B/17/P

9 780985 154899